OVERCOMING DEMONIC SPIDERS AND COBWEBS

A God-Inspired Natural Solution

S. G TREASURE

PUBLISHED BY:

Amazon Kindle Direct Publishing,

Seattle,

Washington DC,

United States.

OVERCOMING DEMONIC SPIDERS AND COBWEBS

A God-Inspired Natural Solution

DEDICATION

This book is dedicated to Almighty God, the giver of life, wisdom, knowledge and understanding.

And to individuals who have been under demonic attack and oppression of the devil for donkey years!

"Behold, I give unto you power to tread on serpents and scorpions, and over all the power of the enemy: and nothing shall by any means hurt you."

-Luke 10:19 (KJV)

ACKNOWLEDGEMENTS

First, my appreciation goes to God Almighty, who gave me the wisdom to write this book. Great thanks to my family for their unrelenting support and contribution towards the success of this book. Many thanks to the love of my life, *Comfort Davids*, for her understanding and support while writing the manuscript of this book.

Senior Evangelist Samson Folarin and *Evangelist Samuel Edunjobi* both deserve special seats in my hall of appreciation. Their selfless guidance and mentoring, which laid the foundation for this book, cannot be left unnoticed.

Lastly, my appreciation goes to the *Wiktionary* (an online dictionary), The *King James' Version* of the Bible, as well as the *Wikipedia*. They all served as reference materials for me while writing the manuscript of this book.

And to others who have in one way or another contributed to the success of this work, I express my profound gratitude and say, "God bless you all." Thank you all.

-**S. G TREASURE**

March 2024.

PREFACE

Demonic spider and cobweb attack is one of the most lethal and devastating spiritual oppression anyone can experience. It doesn't only bring stagnation, setbacks, hatred, and failure at the edge of success to its victims; it also causes disappointments, disfavour, bad-luck, poverty, and the enslavement of the victim's glory. Demonic spider-web attack makes people dead while they are alive.

In view of this, the book **"OVERCOMING DEMONIC SPIDERS AND COBWEBS:** *A God-Inspired Natural Solution*" has been written. The book has been published to help victims of spider-web attacks overcome them through rigorous prayers and the godly use of natural plants. God did not just create natural plants for food but also for the spiritual healing and deliverance of mankind *(Revelation 22:2)*. If natural plants can be used to cure illnesses and diseases, they also carry spiritual properties that can help in tackling certain spiritual problems *(Ezekiel 47:12)*.

Consequently, everyone under the demonic oppression of spider-web attacks will indisputably find this book a useful self-help spiritual guide which brings one out of witchcraft captivity into complete freedom and absolute rest. Welcome on board!

-S.G Treasure

March 2024.

INTRODUCTION

"Then God said, "Let the land produce <u>vegetation</u>: seed-bearing <u>plants</u> and <u>trees</u> on the land that bear fruit with <u>seed</u> in it, according to their various kinds." And it was so. The land produced vegetation: plants bearing seed according to their kinds and trees bearing fruit with seed in it according to their kinds. And God saw that <u>it was good</u>".

-Genesis 1:11-12

God created plants for the use of mankind on the third day of the creation story. However, God looked at every single plant he created and saw that they were good. Unknown to many, God did not just create plants for food but also for healing and the spiritual deliverance of mankind. He deliberately put healing virtues in plants to heal us when we are sick and help us maintain good health at all times. He also deposited spiritual powers in plants to help us tackle, solve, and cure spiritual problems we might be confronted with.

Unfortunately, most Christians only embraced and took advantage of the healing powers and virtues vested in plants but refused to take advantage of the spiritual virtues and powers vested in them. They label the use of plants to solve spiritual problems demonic, while they see it differently when it comes to curing sicknesses and diseases. They forgot God deliberately put spiritual powers in these plants to help us and set us free from all forms of demonic and satanic attacks and oppression. They also forget that some people in the Bible used herbs and plants for various reasons. In fact, the Bible supports the use of herbs and plants for both healing and spiritual liberation.

Sadly, ungodly and satanic people see the spiritual importance of plants more than God's people. Hence, they take massive advantage of them, using them for all sorts of ungodly and selfish purposes. The saddest part is that they even use these plants and herbs to afflict God's people. They use what was initially created to help liberate God's people from spiritual bondage against them. They use these herbs to keep God's people in captivity and oppression.

We cannot entirely blame Christians who have demonised the use of plants to solve spiritual problems. We should blame the ignorance of the early Christians who allowed satanic and demonic people to dominate the use of these plants, and since the spiritual use of plants was and is more common among demonic and fetish people, everyone sees their use to solve spiritual problems as demonic and an occultic practice.

Another side to the narrative is that demonic people invoke fetish, devilish and satanic names into these plants to aid whatever power they already carry to do their bidding. If occultic and demonic people call and chant the names of Satan, demons, and incantations into God-created plants and it works for them, we as Christians can also call the name of the almighty God into them. Calling the name of the one who created those plants into them will indisputably make them superior in terms of effectiveness. We can quote and read Bible verses into them in place of incantations. You will be surprised that it would work more effectively than for occultic and demonic people.

The children of Satan are the ones enjoying the massive spiritual benefits of these plants, while the children of God suffer under their oppression. Satan's children, ironically, are the ones who benefit most from the goodies of God's kingdom and creation.

That is why Jesus says in **Matthew 8:11,** *"And I say unto you, That many shall come from the east and west, and shall sit down with Abraham, Isaac, and Jacob, in the kingdom of heaven. But the children of the kingdom shall be cast out into outer darkness; there shall be weeping and gnashing of teeth."* I now understand better what Jesus Christ meant in the Bible verse above.

In addition to that, **Hosea 4:6** says, *"My people are perished for lack of knowledge."* Many Christians have died from various satanic attacks and oppression due to ignorance. Many destinies are dead and buried while the owners are alive and living, but living in misery, sorrow and pain. Many lives have been caged in satanic captivity for lack of knowledge and ignorance. The sons of the kingdom are wallowing in lack and living miserable lives, living like destitute, while the ungodly people are benefiting heavily from the riches of God's kingdom meant for God's people.

In **Matthew chapter 8,** the centurion *(an unbeliever)* secured instant *"virtual"* healing for his servant, when those who are real children of God could not secure such healing because of their unbelief. That was why Jesus made the statement in Matthew 8:11.

Many Christians have prayed, fasted, and engaged in all sorts of spiritual exercises without any positive result or improvement because not all spiritual problems answer to prayers and fasting. God deliberately put spiritual powers in plants for our use because he knew fasting and prayer alone are sometimes not enough to solve some knotty spiritual problems and issues.

If you allow any witch or occultic person to destroy your destiny or cut off your existence on earth, it is not God's fault. God is not to be blamed. You are to be blamed because God has made provision for everything that you need to set yourself free from any satanic and demonic stronghold or oppression. It is either your ignorance that killed or destroyed you or your religious fanaticism.

Muslims are not the only ones guilty of religious fanatism. We have Christians who are religious fanatics too. Christian fanatics are Christians who interpret Christian tenets and principles to the extreme. Such Christians overdo things and believe plants and herbs that God created for the healing and spiritual deliverance of mankind are evil simply because Satanic and demonic people saw the good in them and decided to take massive advantage of them, even more than God's people.

Yet, these myopic Christians use the same herbs and plants for healing purposes. They make local concoctions to heal themselves of mild sicknesses and diseases, yet they see the same plants as evil! Who are they deceiving? These same Christians go to hospitals for medical examinations and cures. They use medical drugs, yet they label plants and herbs from which those medical drugs are made as demonic. They are only comedians.

The only thing that should be avoided is putting one's trust in these plants over their maker. We should always acknowledge the creator over the created. When you put your trust in these plants and not in God, who created them, problems might arise because God is a jealous God. This is why the use of these plants sometimes does not work for certain people, simply because they put their trust in those plants rather than God, who created them. Hence, if you want all the natural spiritual remedies discussed in this book to work for you, you must first become born again by accepting Jesus Christ into your life. You must trust in the power of God in the plants, not in the plants themselves.

Friends, God is too busy to have time to attend to cases that he has already provided solutions to. He has provided everything you need to enjoy divine health, and that is why we have medical science and other plants with medicinal and curative properties. He has also provided everything you need to enjoy a demonic and oppression-free life through the creation of certain herbs and plants. Only matters that defiles these two should be taken to him in prayers. Only matters beyond all solutions should be taken to him.

Someone might be asking, "Why use plants when the name of Jesus can give you all the protection you need from demonic forces?" I will answer that question by asking another question: "Why did God put powerful healing properties in plants if he wanted the name of Jesus to be the answer to all of life's sicknesses and diseases?" "Why did he bestow the knowledge of medical science on mankind if he wanted the name of Jesus to heal all critical medical problems and complications?"

In conclusion, if you still have negative opinions about the use of plants for spiritual purposes, then you are like *"the son of a cloth seller wearing rags."* This book has thoroughly discussed how to use natural things *(things of nature)* to overcome witchcraft spider and cobweb attacks. At this juncture, it is my prayer that God will use this book to liberate and deliver you permanently from every spiritual and demonic spider and cobweb attack in your life in Jesus' name, irrespective of how fiery and devastating they may be. Once again, welcome on board!

-S.G Treasure

© March 2024.

SECTION A

CHAPTER 1

WHAT ARE DEMONIC COBWEBS AND SPIDERS?

5 "They hatch cockatrice' eggs, and weave the spider's web: he that eateth of their eggs dieth, and that which is crushed breaketh out into a viper. 6 Their webs shall not become garments, neither shall they cover themselves with their works: their works are works of iniquity, and the act of violence is in their hands. 7 Their feet run to evil, and they make haste to shed innocent blood: their thoughts are thoughts of iniquity; wasting and destruction are in their paths. 8 The way of peace they know not; and there is no judgment in their goings: they have made them crooked paths: whosoever goeth therein shall not know peace.

-Isaiah 59:5-8 (KJV)

14 What he trusts in is fragile; what he relies on is a spider's web. 15 He leans on his web, but it gives way; he clings to it, but it does not hold.

-Job 8:14-15 (KJV)

A cobweb is a spider's web. The spider uses its webs to capture and trap other insects for food. However, demonic cobweb attacks are a very serious spiritual problem. Spiritual cobwebs represent spiritual restrictions or limitations placed on an individual to prevent him from moving forward in life.

From the passages above, we could see that cobwebs contain very fragile threads woven by spiders, but as fragile as these webs are, witches can use them to tie an individual spiritually, and it will take the grace of God for the person to break free. Cobweb attacks are part of the weapons and arsenal of witchcraft and marine powers to render people, places, and things desolate. Victims encounter them either in their dreams or physically. These cobwebs and spiders may take over your property, such as your car, your front door, or inside your house or office. Sometimes the attack is not just against an individual alone but against his generation and posterity forever.

Demonic cobweb and spider attacks are anti-breakthrough powers invoked against an individual, usually at the edge of life changing breakthroughs such as academic and career success, marriage, oversees travel, business success, or the acquisition of a profitable job. This is because demonic cobwebs and spiders are usually programmed against the progress and success of witchcraft victims. For instance, the victim could run into cobwebs or see his things covered with cobwebs and spiders days before an important job interview, a marital union, or an important business meeting. These attacks are meant to abort and destroy every good thing that is about to happen in the victim's life.

Cobwebs have a language of their own. Sometimes they form a big "X" on your front door as you come back home. There are certain spiritual experiences that are difficult to believe unless you have experienced them. Sometimes, you discover something like a cobweb rubbing on your face, even in a very clean environment. In fact, people might have been passing through a particular place without experiencing cobwebs, but the moment the victim passes through that place, he will experience them. At times, the victim won't see the cobweb physically, but the impact is felt. This is what is called "invisible spider webs."

Demonic cobweb and spider attacks are witchcraft operations programmed to cause delay or hindrance in a victim's life. Although, it doesn't mean that every cobweb experience is demonic, but when it's becoming a regular and common experience, even on the main road where there are no pillars on which the web can rest, then the victim should brace up for war. The victim should brace up for serious spiritual warfare. The victim should be ready to fight and pray hard. The agenda of demonic cobweb and spider attacks is not different from the central agenda of the devil, as stated in **John 10:10;** which says: *"The thief cometh not but to steal, and to kill, and to* *destroy: I am come that they might have life, and that they might have it more abundantly."*

Demonic cobwebs and spiders remain a veritable spiritual weapon that African spiritual enemies use to deter their victims from progressing in life. This is commonly deployed against people with exceptional glories and bright futures. It happens mostly to those with a bright future. Demonic cobwebs are very real. What can one make out of a situation where one is among many people walking shoulder to shoulder only to feel thick cobwebs across one's forehead while the rest feel nothing? And that continues like that for, like, three times in a day?

In some advanced cases, the victim sees spiders all around him and everywhere he goes. Sometimes, spiders from nowhere drop on the victim's body at any location. Every corner of the victim's room could be filled with spiders entrapped in their webs. When it reaches this stage, the victim might need a miracle to be free. If the victim wants to leave the house and picks up his shirt, spiders will crawl out of the shirt. If he picks up his shoes to wear, spiders will crawl out again. This is about the highest level of this demonic oppression anyone can face. But, I assure you, in the name of Jesus, you shall be free after carrying out all the God-inspired natural solutions as well as spiritual assignments mentioned in this book.

A cobweb attack is a witchcraft weapon used by "household" enemies, i.e., witchcraft attacks from members of one's family, relatives, neighbours, friends, and well-wishers. When a satanic cobweb strikes a person, it causes stagnation and demotion. Just as the insects trapped in a real-life cobweb are held down and helpless, that is how the victim will be trapped and unable to move forward in life.

Unfortunately, the more the insect tries to set itself free, the more the spider spins more cobwebs around it to prevent it from securing its freedom. When the insect tries and tries and is unable to get out of the web, it gives up and resigns to fate. When this happens, the spider comes around and feasts on the helpless insect.

The same thing applies to demonic spiders and cobwebs; it is just that, in this case, the victim is not an insect but a human being. When a victim of demonic cobwebs gets entangled, it holds him down, preventing him from making any further progress in life. The victim is trapped and held hostage. The more he tries to set himself free, either through fasting or prayers, the more the satanic spiders represented by witches spin more cobwebs around him till he becomes helpless and gives up. At that point, other spiritual spiders (the witches) gather to feast on the victim, either by sharing and drinking his blood or eating his flesh.

But the good news is that there is a way out. With the help of Jesus Christ and the spiritual instructions outlined in this book, freedom from every demonic cobweb and spider is certain. For everyone already entangled in demonic cobwebs, your time of freedom has come. For victims of Satanic cobweb to be free, a higher power is required, which is the power of Jesus Christ.

From another perspective, to dream of cobwebs is a bad omen. It buries a man's glory while he is alive and hinders his movement and progress in life. It invokes the spirit of backwardness that makes a person count losses more often than gains. A person under the curse of the household cobweb will struggle to get a breakthrough but never get it until the blessings expire. The person may not experience a cobweb attack until something good comes his way.

Someone under the bondage of cobweb is like a person trapped in a prison or cage with satanic devises. To break the bondage, it is through rigorous prayers and certain godly spiritual assignments. You need to deal with them so that you can become what God wants you to be. Cobweb and spider attacks operate via satanic monitoring gadgets, which monitor the progress of their victims and manipulate them from trying to get free. They disrupt the victim's life, making him miss his blessings and vulnerable to ill-luck, failure, frustration, and stagnation. The plight of the victim of a cobweb monitoring spirit can be explained as that of a person who has a rope tied to one of his legs. Anytime he makes a move, the rope is pulled, and he falls down and is unable to progress. It is also like a situation whereby the victim's life is under remote control.

People under cobweb monitoring spirits are known as blind witches in the witchcraft circle, but they are actually spiritual slaves in real life. These are people who can no longer live authentic lives. They experience failure, stagnation, hatred, promise and failure, ill-luck, a spirit of dishonour and frustration, etc. The spirit of cobwebs is a weapon of witchcraft deployed to harass its victims until they become frustrated and begin to backslide from the Christian faith.

Victims also often experience being pressed down during sleep, eating or having sexual intercourse in dreams, being unable to climb or descend the hill, writing examinations in an old school, picking snails, and meeting cobwebs physically, among other bad spiritual experiences. If one is under the manipulation of the monitoring spirit, it implies that such a person has a good and glorious destiny, which the devil is trying to steal, kill, or destroy **(John 10:10).**

In a nutshell, cobweb and spider attacks are witchcraft weapons used to enslave the glory, lives, and destinies of the innocent. Witches use cobweb and spider attacks to achieve a number of evil objectives. We shall be perusing these evil objectives, and they include the following:

REASONS WITCHES USE COBWEB AND SPIDERS TO ATTACK PEOPLE

1. To cause stagnation in their victim's life.

2. To cause setbacks.

3. To bring failure at the hedge of success to their victims.

4. To cause unnatural and unnecessary delay.

5. To bring series of disappointment in their victims ways.

6. To divert the blessings and breakthroughs of their victims.

7. To cause loss of divine connections.

8. To tie down their victim's destiny and make it stagnant.

9. To enslave their victim's spiritual life.

10. To shield their victim from helpers of destiny.

11. To cause disfavour and bad-luck to their victims such that they experience big time disappointments.

12. To cause hatred in victims life, especially from destiny helpers.

13. To make their victims remain single for life as suitor may never see the real them but a different them that is not marriageable.

14. To cause division in their victim's marriage and make their spouses to turn against them.

15. To cause business breakdown, loss in sales and even increase debt in their victim's life and business.

16. To deny their victims the opportunity to get lucrative jobs even though they passed the interview.

17. To hinder or slow down the progress of their victims.

18. To cause slow growth in the church as a pastor.

19. To make good members to turn against the pastor in a church.

20. To make ministerial helpers stop helping a pastor.

21. To cover their victim's spiritual gifts so that it will not manifest or people will not recognize or appreciate such gifts.

22. To make their victim's spiritual life to be below average.

23. To cause cause miscarriages in victim's marriage.

24. To control victim's life and destiny.

25. To capture their victims spiritually and make them a slave.

26. To imprison their victims and eventually sacrifice them on their altar.

27. To render their victims useless in life.

28. To inject sickness or disease into their victim's life that can't be medically detected or cured.

29. To project future failure into their victim's life.

30. To tie their victim's destiny to failure and poverty.

31. To open up their victim's life for satanic attacks and oppression.

32. To initiate their victims into witchcraft society.

33. To cause contract or project failure in their victim's life.

34. To control their victim's spirit and subject it to their control. *(To remote control their victim's life)*.

35. To make their victims a blind witch i.e. a slave of witchcraft via drinking, smoking, negative excessive lifestyle etc.

36. To afflict their victim's family.

37. To control their victim's mind and use it at will. *(Mind-controlling powers)*.

38. To make their victims dead while alive.

39. To make their victims to be alive but treated as dead and completely forgotten by others.

40. To make their victim a walking corpse.

41. To manipulate their victim into wrong places for deliverance.

42. To manipulate their victims by making true friends and destiny helpers appear as enemies.

43. To manipulate their victims by making real time enemies appear as friends and destiny helpers.

44. To lure their victims into evil marriages.

45. To mislead their victims in life.

46. To divert their victims away from their real purpose in life.

47. To put acute fear in their captives.

48. To make their victim's glory useless and unusable.

49. To cause false accusations for their victims.

50. To share the body and blood of their victims spiritual and kill them.

AREAS OF TARGET FOR DEMONIC COBWEBS AND SPIDERS

1. Your forehead, which represents your star: When cobwebs attack your forehead, your glory is being tampered with. Your glory has been enslaved. You will just be working without anything to show for it. The glory that God gave you at birth has been changed and traded on the witchcraft altar.

2. Your eyes, which represent your vision: When demonic cobwebs attack your eyes, it affects your vision. You might not be able to think straight or reason logically again. You might begin to see things with a different eye and from a different perspective. Your perception of things and issues will change to suit the agenda of witchcraft spirits controlling your life, which helps them destroy you faster.

3. Your mouth, which represents your destiny: Haven't you heard the proverb, "A closed mouth is a closed destiny?" When witchcraft cobwebs attack your mouth, you find it difficult to pray the way you should. The influence of your mouth as regards the events in your life is reduced. You might not be able to use your mouth and the words that come out of it to rescue yourself or for your own benefit.

4. Your face, which represents your glory: When witchcraft spiders or cobwebs attack your face, they wear on your face an evil mask. They put an evil mark on your face, which makes it difficult for destiny helpers to locate or see you, and if they see you, they will be unwilling to help you. If the victim is unmarried, the attack can keep him or her unmarried for life because prospective suitors or wives will be seeing something different. They might either be seeing a masquerade or a demon in his or her face. Such an evil mask can even scare away quality people from the victim's life.

5. Your hand, which represents your work or handiwork: Victims of cobweb and spider attacks hardly prosper in their work. When cobwebs attack the hand of an individual, that person's work will begin to suffer. Clients and customers will prefer to patronise your competitors, even when your product or service is the best.

Conclusively, victims of spiritual spiders and cobwebs need to pray and, at the same time, carry out all the spiritual assignments listed in this book if they really want to be free. We shall end this chapter with serious and aggressive prayers. This is because only rigorous prayers, coupled with some spiritual assignments, can set you free. Therefore, if you are not born again yet, you might need to give your life to Christ so that whatever prayer we pray or any spiritual assignment we embark on in this book can work for you. In the mean time, pray the following prayers with anger and aggression:

PRAYER POINTS AGAINST WITCHCRAFT SPIDERS AND COBWEBS

1. *I command every demonic cobweb assigned against my life and destiny be destroyed in Jesus' name.*

2. *Every attacker of my goodness through cobwebs and spiders be destroyed in the name of Jesus.*

3. *Every patrolling spiders and cobweb assigned against my life and business be paralyzed, in Jesus' name.*

4. *Every suspended power using spiders and cobweb against my life, collide with the rock of ages and die in the name of Jesus.*

5. *Anything deposited in my life and body through cobwebs and its spiders, be destroyed in the name above all names.*

6. *Any man or woman using cobwebs and spiders as an access to enter my life, fall down and die, in the name of Jesus.*

7. *Every net of demonic cobweb placed upon my head melt away in Jesus' name.*

8. *I command every demonic chain of cobweb placed upon my hands, legs, neck and waist to break and be destroyed in the name of Jesus.*

9. *Father, Lord let every evil checkpoints of satanic cobwebs mounted against my life and goodness be dismantled by the power of the Holy Ghost in the name of Jesus.*

10. *Blood of Jesus, purify me from the effect of every demonic cobwebs that I have accidentally run into Jesus' name.*

11. *I command day and night to turn against any man or woman, spirit or agent spreading cobwebs to arrest my goodness in the name of Jesus.*

12. *Every household strongman using cobweb to block my way be wasted in Jesus' name.*

13. *Every witchcraft spider flying contrary to my destiny fall down and die.*

14. *Every wicked spider installed against me be overthrown in the name of Jesus.*

15. *Every hostile person who wants to imprison my wealth with cobwebs I bindfold you in Jesus' name.*

16. *Every cobweb spirit attached to my life and destiny, I bind and cast you out, in the name of Jesus.*

17. Cobweb attack of poverty and backwardness over my life, receive fire, burn to ashes, in the name of Jesus.

18. Spiritual and physical cobweb of hindrances following me about, I set you on fire, burn to ashes, in the name of Jesus.

19. Any trap set for me by cobweb begin to catch your owners, in the name of Jesus. (Pray it well)

20. Blood of Jesus, flush out every satanic cobweb and evil net tying me down somewhere, in the name of Jesus.

SECTION B

OVERCOMING DEMONIC SPIDERS AND COBWEBS

(A God-Inspired Natural Solution)

... and the leaves of the tree were for the healing of the nations.

-Revelation 22:2

The passage above also corroborates the claim that God created plants for physical and spiritual healing of mankind. Plants have not been created for food only. **Psalm 104:14 (KJV)** says: *"He causeth the grass to grow for the cattle, And <u>herb for the service of man</u>: That he may bring forth food out of the earth; And wine that maketh glad the heart of man, And oil to make his face to shine, and bread which strengtheneth man's heart."*

There are many instances in the Bible where things of nature have been used either to heal or perform miracles *(spiritual deliverance).* In **2 Kings 20,** Hezekiah was sick and was unto death. Prophet Isaiah came to him to deliver God's message to him, telling him to put his house as he was going to die. But, Hezekiah turned his face to the wall and prayed to the LORD, reminding God how he had walked blamelessly before him in truth and with a perfect heart and how he had done that which was good in the sight of God. Hezekiah said these words with tears.

God was moved and spoke to Isaiah again. Isaiah had not left the middle of Hezekiah's court when God spoke to him. God told Isaiah to turn back and return to Hezekiah. God told him to tell Hezekiah that he had heard his prayers and seen his tears, that he would heal him in three days, and that he would add an additional fifteen (15) years to his years. God then instructed Isaiah to take a lump of fig and prepare a poultice of figs from it. God told Isaiah to lay it on Hezekiah's boils, and immediately that was done. Hezekiah recovered and was healed.

God could have just asked Isaiah to pray for Hezekiah, and he would be healed, but God decided to use a plant *(a fig tree)*, a product of nature, to heal Hezekiah. Poultice of figs refers to juice secreted by the fig tree, which contains a very effective enzyme against calluses and warts. To heal Hezekiah, all Isaiah did was cut fig leaves and apply their juice twice a day to Hezekiah's warts and calluses to remove them.

Also, in **2 Kings 2:19**, some men of a certain city came to Elisha for help concerning the bad water in their city; the water was bitter and unfit for drinking. Elisha asked the men to bring him a container with salt. He went to the spring of water, cast the salt there, and commanded the water to be healed. Immediately, the water was healed and fit for drinking. Sometimes, God uses things of nature to perform miracles and spiritual healings.

In another instance, Naman, who was the commander of the army of Syria in **2 Kings 5,** was directed by prophet Elisha to go to the river Jordan and wash himself in the river seven times, and his leprosy would disappear. But, Naaman refused to carry out the spiritual instruction. He considered it disgraceful for a person of his calibre to be bathing in a dirty local river like that of Jordan. But, the little girl who advised him initially to seek help from Israel implored him to give it a try, which he did, and his leprosy disappeared,.His skin became like that of a newborn baby.

I know if a prophet tells many of us today to go to a river and have a river bath in order to secure our freedom from spiritual oppression, we will never agree, we will never listen, nor obey. Some of us will label the prophet fetish and demonic. But, in the Bible days, stream or river baths were never demonic; many miracles were associated with pools, streams, or river baths.

There was even a place in the scriptures, precisely in the New Testament, where an angel would come down and stir up a particular pool *(the pool of Bethesda)*, and whoever first stepped into it would be healed **(John 5:1– 15).** But, all that has changed today. We have forgotten that God can use anything, including the things of nature, to perform his miracles. All the wars and battles the Israelites fought on their way to promise land followed different spiritual approaches. But the modern day Christian wants God to solve all his spiritual problems through only one means, and that is through fasting and praying. Unfortunately, God does not work like that.

All of these epistles are to prepare our minds that God works in mysterious ways. We cannot put God in a box and expect him to act only in a certain way. You cannot expect God to become stereotyped and act in a certain way all of the time. If you think all spiritual problems will answer to only fasting and prayers, then you are only deceiving yourself. If you belong to a Christian denomination that believes fasting and praying are the only solutions to all spiritual problems, then you may have to re-examine your membership.

This is because God works in mysterious ways. His ways are too dynamic and unpredictable. There were instances in the Bible where Jesus refused to pray for those who came to him for healing. In one particular instance, a man born blind from birth received his sight through a completely different means than prayers. Jesus only spat on the ground, made mud from the spit, and put the mud on the blind man's eyes, using the mud to annoint his eyes. He further instructed the blind man to go to the river Siloam to wash off the mud, and he would receive his sight. The man obeyed and followed the spiritual instructions of Jesus, and he regained his sight **(John 9:1–7 KJV)**.

In **Genesis 9:3 (KJV),** God said; *"Every moving thing that liveth shall be meat for you; even as the green herb, I have given you all thing"*. Truly, God has given us all things. While creating the world, God made sure he provided everything we would need to make our stay on earth enjoyable, comfortable, and problem-free. Every plant, herb, and natural thing that God created carries nutritional, healing, and spiritual properties to make our stay on earth a heaven-on-earth experience. It's just that we refuse to discover them. While some discovered them, but refused to take full advantage of their benefits.

In **Hebrew 6:7 (KJV)** God says; *"For the earth which drinketh in the rain that cometh oft upon it, and bringeth forth herbs meet for them by whom it is dressed, receiveth blessing from God"*. Mankind has received great blessings from God in the form of plants, herbs, and natural things created by Him. But many people are oblivious to this. That is why I said in the introduction that if you allow any witch to kill you, it is not God's fault, because God has provided everything you need to defend yourself spiritually against all oppressions of the evil one. It was you who refused to take advantage of them because of your religious fanaticism and ignorance.

In conclusion, **Ezekiel 47:12 (KJV)** says; *"And by the river upon the bank thereof, on this side and on that side, shall grow all trees for meat, whose leaf shall not fade, neither shall the fruit thereof be consumed: it shall bring forth new fruit according to his months, because their waters they issued out of the sanctuary: and the fruit thereof shall be for meat, and the <u>leaf thereof for medicine</u>."*

As I conclude, I repeat again that God has fully done his part. He has provided everything we need to survive in this wicked and sinister world. He has provided all that we need to live good lives here. But, many believers still suffer because of ignorance. It is the children of Satan who enjoy all the goodies and riches of His creation.

However, in the subsequent chapters of this book, we shall begin to look at about four different spiritual assignments which we can undertake in order to combat and overcome witchcraft spider and cobweb attacks in our lives, such that we will be totally free from them eternally.

Consequently, if one of the remedies is not producing the desired result for you, kindly try another one. I know that by the time you try all four demonic spider and cobweb attacks in your life will cease forever. I pray as you embark on these spiritual exercises, God, in his infinite mercy, will use them to end witchcraft and demonic oppression in your life forever, in Jesus' name (Amen).

CHAPTER TWO

THE SPIRITUAL EFFICACY OF SCENT LEAVES

(Ocimum Gratissimum)

Ocimum gratissimum, also known as clove basil, African basil, or wild basil, is a species of Ocimum. It is native to Africa, Madagascar, southern Asia, and the Bismarck Archipelago and naturalised in Polynesia, Hawaii, Mexico, Panama, the West Indies, Brazil, and Bolivia. Other names of Ocimum Gratissimum according to different languages, tribes, and countries include the following:

It is called *"Efinrin" in Yoruba Land. It is called "Tchayo" in Fon, Benin. It is known as "Daidoya" in Hausa. Its Igbo name is "Nchuawu." It is called "Ntonng" in Ibibio. "Fobazen" in Haiti. "Kunudiri" in Okrika. "Yerba di holé" in Papiamento. It is generally known as "Clove Basil" and "African Basil," while in Hawaii it is known as "Wild Basil."*

Scent leaf is known as *"Ebe-amwonkho" in Edo. "Dogosui" in Ewe. "Tamwõtswãgi" in Nupe. "Kpan-sroh" in the Irigwe language. "Añyeba" in Igala. "Ntong" in Ibibio, Efik. "Kunudiri" in Kirikeni Okuein. "Nunum" in Akan. "Nunu Bush" in Jamaica (from the Akan language). "Vaayinta" (వాయింట) in Telugu, and "Maduruthala" in Sri Lanka.*

Scent leaf *(Ocimum gratissimum)* is a homegrown shrub commonly found in farms, gardens, and other tropical areas. It is commonly used as a spice for cooking delicacies due to its aromatic smell and taste. It is called a "scent leaf" because it carries a unique scent (smell), which can be used as seasoning to spice up a vegetable soup. It gives meals that delightful, unique, and sweet taste and aroma. Any meal with a scent leaf will definitely get your mouth watering.

But there is more to scent leaf than its food properties. It can also be used to cure certain diseases. Scent leaf is very rich in nutrients and essential oils; it can be useful in the treatment of microbial infections, cough, cancer, diarrhoea, anaemia, inflammatory diseases, and so on.

If you live in an area or country where it is hard to find scent leaves, you can order them from Amazon, eBay, or other online stores across the world. Just search on Google writing: "where can I order scent leaf from?" and it will bring up a host of online stores where you can order from. The only difference is that it is the dried one that will be sent to you. But, whether dried or fresh, a scent leaf is a scent leaf. This doesn't diminish its efficacy and power.

However, in this chapter, our aim and purpose are solely to discuss the major spiritual powers embedded in this leaf by God and how we can use them to our benefit. The purpose is to outline the major spiritual properties the creator has put in this particular plant for the liberation of mankind. They include the following:

SPIRITUAL BENEFITS OF OCIMUM GRATISSIMUM (SCENT LEAF)

1. It shields you from witchcraft spiders and cobweb attacks.

2. It prevents and protects you from witchcraft marks made on people's bodies overnight.

3. It clears your path from evil blockage by demonic agents.

4. It removes witchcraft invisible marks from your body.

5. It prevents evil dreams and witchcraft manipulations from your life.

6. It drives evil spirits and witchcraft presence away from your houses and dwellings.

7. It prevents witchcraft monitoring spirit from monitoring your life and progress.

8. It keeps evil people far from you.

9. It cancels out witchcraft spells as well as curses from devilish people.

10. It destroys generational curses.

11. It breaks the stronghold of stagnation and delay in your life.

12. It heals you of any spiritual injury or attack.

13. You become spiritually unavailable for destruction by the enemy.

UNIQUE WAYS THROUGH WHICH SCENT LEAF CAN BE USED TO ACHIEVE ALL OF THE ABOVE

(A) SCENT LEAF BATH

Instruction: *Carry out this spiritual assignment every night for 7 days. Do this assignment around 9:00.p.m when you are not going out again. Also, never carry out this assignment during your period (monthly cycle) and abstain from sex during the period of this spiritual exercise.*

Needed Items: *A reasonable quantity of fresh or dry scent leaves, water, cooking pot, cooking gas or stove, salt, a bathing bucket.*

Procedure:

• *Get a reasonable quantity of scent leaves.*

• *Rinse them in a clean water.*

• *Put them in a pot, add water (water that is enough to take a bath with).*

• *Add little salt.*

• *Put the pot which has the scent leaves and water on the fire.*

• *Boil for like 30 minutes.*

• *After boiling for 30 minutes, the water will change from white to brownish colour, put the pot down, let the water cool off.*

• *After that, remove the scent leaves from the boiled water.*

• *Pour the boiled scent leaf water in an empty bucket (Do not additional water. That is why I said earlier that the water you put on the fire must be enough for you to bathe with).*

• *Read Psalms 24, 35, 69 and 109 into the scent leaf water.*

• *Then pray into the water as led by the holy spirit. (You can choose prayer points from those at the end of this chapter).*

• *After praying, take the scent leaf water to the bathroom for bath.*

• *Only rinse your entire body with the water, don't use soap or sponge.*

• *As you bath with the water, speak into your life. Say the things you want and those you don't want. Ask God to make you immuned to Satanic spider and cobweb attacks.*

• *After bathing, don't towel your body. Let the water dry on your body.*

• *While waiting for the scent leaf water to dry on your body, pray more and more.*

• *After the scent leaf water has dried up, you go to bed.*

• *Repeat the process for 7 days.*

By the grace of God, you will never experience cobweb or spider attacks again. This is a big mystery of God. The spiritual virtues that God puts in scent leaves are so powerful that witches and wizards can't fathom. When you bathe regularly with scent-leaf water, it keeps evil people far from you.

The spiritual power of the scent leaf, which is contained in your bathing water, diffuses into your skin and body. Now, even at home or outside, evil people or people with bad intentions will always keep their distance from you. All spells and curses of evil and jealous people would be broken. When you observe a delay or stagnation in your life, try as quickly as you can to bathe with boiled scent leaf water.

Likewise, a boiled-scent leaf water bath heals you of any spiritual injury or attack from a person who does not mean any good for you. If you notice any strange mark, pain, or hot sensation on any part of your body and you are sure you did not scratch yourself anywhere, you should consider a scent leaf bath immediately. Do not wait until things get out of hand; prevention is better than cure.

Those who regularly bathe with scent-leaf water become spiritually unavailable for destruction. When someone tries to attack you, they will quickly find out that you are a no go area. This is because of your scent-leaf bath. They will seek you but will not find you. This makes it impossible for them to harm you or hurt you spiritually.

Remember, I said you should speak into your life while taking this bath. You need to offer prayer to God Almighty, who is the protector himself. It is God who puts power in the scent leaf, so don't see the leaf as your saviour. If you idolise the leaf, God might hinder the whole process from working for you because God is a jealous God. You don't worship things created while you ignore the creator, who is the real source.

Whoever is secured by God has a guaranteed safety forever. So while taking your bath, open your mouth and pray, telling God what you want from him. God is too faithful to fail and will never fail you now. Amen.

(B) OTHER USES OF SCENT LEAVES

• *To remove negative energy around your house, shop, office, or business place, use boiled scent leaf water to mop the floor of your house, shop, office, or business place.*

• *To remove demonic and evil presence in your home, office, or business place, get the particles of scent leaves you got from your scent leaf water, put them in a tray, and keep them in your house, office, or business place. You will never feel any demonic presence in your space again. Scent leaves drive away evil spirits and demons.*

• *When you constantly have evil dreams, do a scent leaf bath. When you constantly have dreams of eating food in the dream, squeeze a small portion of scent leaves with water and pray into it. Read Psalm 69 into it to cancel every evil deposit the enemy must have deposited into your system through eating in the dream, then drink the scent-leaf water. It will destroy all the negative effects of the food eaten in the dream and neutralise its powers. If you drink scent-leaf water regularly, eating in the dream will stop permanently. Witches will stop bringing you evil poison in dreams.*

• If you notice that your finances are being attacked by witchcraft powers, get a small quantity of scent leaves. Put the leaves in a bottle of anointing oil (Olive oil). Pray on it daily for three days. Let it ferment very well. You can add fasting if you have the capacity to. Read Psalm 35 into it each day. On the third day, start using it. Use it to rub your palms and head every morning. Your head signifies your glory. You will notice a drastic change in your finances after this exercise.

• If demonic spiders have taken over your home, house, and properties, such that you see spiders in the dream, in real life, they crawl out of your body, clothes, and belongings; they just appear from nowhere to attack you, etc. Then, do a scent leaf bath regularly. Also, clean your home and house with scent-leaf water to banish negative energy. Also, gather particles of scent leaves you gather from your scent bath, put them in a tray, and keep them in your house. You can also rub scent-leaf-soaked perfume on your head, hands, and feet. Do all these for 7 days, and all the spiders will disappear within 7 days of the use of these items. You will no longer suffer spider attacks ever again. Ever!

POSSIBLE PRAYER POINTS TO SUPPORT THE ABOVE SPIRITUAL ASSIGNMENTS

(Ask God for forgiveness of sins, the sins of your fathers, mothers and ancestors. Put your middle finger in the water and sanctify it in the name of Jesus).

1. Put you right middle finger into the scent leaf water and say): Every spider and cobweb spirit attached to my life and destiny, loose your grip as i undergo this bath in the name of Jesus.

2. Cobweb attack of poverty and backwardness over my life, die as I undertake this bath in the name of Jesus.

3. Spiritual and physical cobweb of hindrances following me about, I wash you away through this water in the name of Jesus. Every trap set for me by cobweb begin to catch your owners in the name of Jesus. (Pray it well)

4. I turn this water into the Blood of Jesus, flush out every satanic cobweb and evil net tying me down on one spot in the name of Jesus. (Pray it 7 times)

5. Blood of Jesus silence everything scattering my favor and finances, in the name of Jesus.

6. My Father, let any man or woman of darkness using cobwebs as a means to enter my life, let them become frustrated in the name of Jesus.

7. *Satanic cobwebs attack of "nobody can ever favor me" , be destroyed in the name of Jesus. (Pray it with enough is enough spirit)*

8. *Cobweb attack of evil and destiny killers, waiting for me at the season of my blessings be wasted in the name of Jesus. (Declare it well)*

9. *O God, re-connect me back to all the places satanic cobweb have disconnected me from, in the name of Jesus. (Pray it well that woman)*

10. *I command every demonic cobweb placed upon my hands, legs, head, neck and waist to destroyed in the name of Jesus.*

11. *My Father, Let any strange man or woman manipulating my life and marital destiny with cobwebs, be destroyed in the name of Jesus.*

12. *My Father, let every witchcraft cobweb from any stubborn personality in my household, be destroyed as I take this bath in the name of Jesus.*

13. *Every satanic cobweb assigned to divert me from the path of my breakthrough be swallowed in the name of Jesus. (Your freedom has come)!!!*

14. *Cobweb of no way!!! set against my blessings and favor be destroyed by the blood of Jesus.*

15. Powers of my father's house and mother's house that are sending invisible cobweb against me, I bind you in the name of Jesus.

16. Blood of Jesus, use this water to purify me from every effect of household spiders and cobwebs that I might have come in contact with, in the name of Jesus.

17. Cobweb and spider of hardship, poverty and rejection over my life, as I take this bath, loose your hold over my life in Jesus' name.

18. Father Lord, let day and night turn against any man or woman, spirit or agent spreading cobwebs to arrest my goodness, in the name of Jesus.

19. Every household strongman using cobweb to block my way, melt away as I carry out this spiritual instruction in Jesus' name.

21. Embargo of nobody can ever favor (mention your name) over my life, waste away as I undertake this task.

22. Father Lord, let every evil checkpoints of satanic cobwebs mounted against my life and goodness be dismantled by the Holy Ghost bulldozer, in the name of Jesus.

23. Thank you Lord because you have answered my prayers, for in Jesus' name I pray. (AMEN)

CHAPTER THREE

THE SPIRITUAL SIGNIFICANCE OF LANTANA CAMARA

Lantana camara is a flowering ornamental plant belonging to the family Verbenaceae. It has a smell similar to that of the scent leaf (Ocimum gratissimum), but a major difference between Lantana camara and the scent leaf is that lantana has ornamental flowers and small greenish berries as fruits. The plant also carries spiritual power that can put a permanent end to witchcraft spider and cobweb attacks on an individual.

The plant is called "Ewonadele" in Yoruba, "Kimbamahalba" in Hausa, and "Anya nnunu" in Igbo. It is also known as "Red Sage," "Shrub Verbena," or "Yellow Sage" in Kannada. To know the local name of the plant in your country, do not hesitate to go on Google and search.

Although I have included the picture of the plant at the top of the page, you can recognise it when you see it.

According to research, the plant is said to contain anti-bacterial, anti-fungal, wound healing, anti-motility, anti-ulcerogenic, hemolytic, anti+hyperglycemic, anti-filarial, anti-inflammatory, embryotoxicity, anti-urolithiatic, anti-cancer and anti-proliferative, anti-mutagenic, anti-oxidant, and mosquito-controlling properties.

Lantana camara might not be an edible plant like a scent leaf, as research has shown that its berries (fruits) can be poisonous. But it is safe to bathe with its water. However, in this chapter, our aim and purpose are solely to discuss the major spiritual powers embedded in this leaf by God and how we can use them to our benefit. The purpose is to outline the major spiritual properties the creator has put in this particular plant for the liberation of mankind. They include the following:

SPIRITUAL BENEFITS OF LANTANA CAMARA

1. It shields you from witchcraft spiders and cobweb attacks.

2. It prevents and protects you from witchcraft marks made on people's bodies overnight.

3. It clears your path from evil blockage by demonic agents.

4. It removes witchcraft invisible marks from your body.

5. It prevents evil dreams and witchcraft manipulations from your life.

6. It drives evil spirits and witchcraft presence away from your houses and dwellings.

7. It prevents witchcraft monitoring spirit from monitoring your life and progress.

8. It keeps evil people far from you.

9. It cancels out witchcraft spells as well as curses from devilish people.

10. It destroys generational curses.

11. It breaks the stronghold of stagnation and delay in your life.

12. It heals you of any spiritual injury or attack.

13. You become spiritually unavailable for destruction by the enemy.

UNIQUE WAYS THROUGH WHICH LANTANA CAMARA LEAF CAN BE USED TO ACHIEVE ALL OF THE ABOVE

(A) LANTANA CAMARA LEAF BATH

Instruction: *Carry out this spiritual assignment every night for 7 days. Do this assignment around 9:00.p.m when you* are not going out again. Also, never carry out this assignment during your period (monthly cycle) and abstain from sex during the period of this spiritual exercise.

Needed Items: *A reasonable quantity of fresh or dry Lantana Camara leaves, water, cooking pot, cooking gas or stove, salt, a bathing bucket.*

Procedure:

• *Get a reasonable quantity of Lantana Camara leaves.*

• *Rinse them in a clean water.*

• *Put them in a pot, add water (water that is enough to take a bath with).*

• *Add a little salt.*

• *Put the pot which has the Lantana Camara leaves and water on the fire.*

• *Boil for like 30 minutes.*

• *After boiling for 30 minutes, the water will change from white brownish colour, put the pot down, let the water cool off.*

• *After that, remove the Lantana leaves from the boiled water.*

• *Pour the boiled Lantana leaf water in an empty bucket (Do not additional water. That is why I said earlier that the water you put on the fire must be enough for you to bathe with)*

• Read Psalms 24, 35, 69 and 109 into the Lantana leaf water.

• Then pray into the water as led by the holy spirit (You can choose prayer points from those at the end of this chapter).

• After praying, take the Lantana leaf water to the bathroom for bath.

• Only rinse your entire body with the water, don't use soap or sponge.

• As you bath with the water, speak into your life. Say the things you want and those you don't want. Ask God to make you immuned to Satanic spider and cobweb attacks.

• After bathing, don't towel your body. Let the water dry on your body.

• While waiting for the Lantana leaf water to dry on your body, pray more and more.

• After the Lantana leaf water has dried up on your body, you go to bed.

• Repeat the process for 7 days.

By the grace of God, you will never experience cobweb or spider attacks never again. This is a big mystery of God. The spiritual virtues that God put in Lantana leaves is so powerful that witches and wizards can't fathom. When you bath regularly with Lantana leaf water, it keeps evil people far from you.

The spiritual power of the Lantana leaf which is contained in your bathing water diffuses into your skin and body. Now, even at home or outside, evil people or people with bad intentions will always keep their distance from you. All spells and curses of evil and jealous people would be broken. When you observe a delay or stagnation in your life, try as quickly as you can to bathe with boiled Lantana leaf water.

Likewise, boiled Lantana leaf water bath heals you of any spiritual injury or attack from a person who does not mean any good for you. If you notice any strange mark, pain or hot sensation on any part of your body and you are sure you did not scratch yourself anywhere, you should consider a Lantana leaf bath immediately. Do not wait until things get out of hand, prevention is better than cure.

Those who regularly bathe with Lantana leaf water become spiritually unavailable for destruction. When someone tries to attack you, they will quickly find out that you are a no go area. This is because of your Lantana leaf bath. They will seek you but will not find you. This makes it impossible for them to harm or hurt you spiritually.

Remember I said you should speak into your life while taking this bath. Yes, it should be a form of prayer to God Almighty who is the protector himself. It is God who put power in Lantana leaf, so don't see the leaf as your saviour. If you idolise the leaf, God might hinder the whole process from working for you because God is a jealous God. You don't worship things created while you leave the creator, who is the source.

Whoever is secured by God has a guaranteed safety forever. So while taking your bath, open your mouth and pray, telling God what you want from him. God is too faithful to fail and will never fail you now. Amen.

(B) OTHER USES OF LANTANA LEAVES

• *To remove negative energy around your house, shop, office or business place, use boiled Lantana leaf water to mop the floor of your house, shop, office or business place.*

• *To remove demonic and evil presence in your home, office or business place, get the particles of Lantana leaves you got from your Lantana leaf water, put them in a tray and keep them in your house, office or business place. You will never feel any demonic presence in your space again. Lantana leaves drives away evil spirits and demons.*

•If you notice that your finances are being attacked by witchcraft powers, get a small quantity of Lantana camara leaves. Put the leaves in a bottle of anointing oil (Olive oil). Pray on it daily for three days. Let it ferment very well. You can add fasting if you have the capacity to. Read Psalm 35 into it each day. On the third day, start using it. Use it to rub your palms and head every morning. Your head signifies your glory. You will notice a drastic change in your finances after this exercise.

• If demonic spiders have taken over your home, house, and properties, such that you see spiders in the dream, in real life, they crawl out of your body, clothes, and belongings; they just appear from nowhere to attack you, etc. Then, do a Lantana leaf bath regularly. Also, clean your home and house with Lantana-leaf water to banish negative energy. Also, gather particles of Lantana leaves you gather from your Lantana bath, put them in a tray, and keep them in your house. You can also rub Lantana-leaf-soaked perfume on your head, hands, and feet. Do all these for 7 days, and all the spiders will disappear within 7 days of the use of these items. You will no longer suffer spider attacks ever again. Ever!

POSSIBLE PRAYER POINTS TO SUPPORT THE ABOVE SPIRITUAL ASSIGNMENTS

(Ask God for forgiveness of sins, the sins of your fathers, mothers and ancestors. Put your middle finger in the water and sanctify it in the name of Jesus).

1. Any sin that my parents and ancestors committed, that gave room for spiritual attacks to operate fully in my life, be washed away by the blood of Jesus.

2. Blood of Jesus, mix with this water to wash away every evil mark of hatred and cobwebs in my life and body.

3. Cobweb attack of missed opportunity attacking me day and night, suffer destruction in the name of Jesus

4. Every evil ever done to me through cobweb attacks, be reversed in the name of Jesus

5. Let the thunder of God locate and dismantle every witchcraft power using cobweb to fire afflictions into my life in the name of Jesus.

6. Witchcraft cobweb covering my glory from being noticed by my helpers, loose your hold over me completely in the name of Jesus.

7. Every power that want me to die in this condition, you are a liar, die, in Jesus name

8. Every dark power that is monitoring me, receive blindness in Jesus name

9. Every power assigned to change my destiny, die, in Jesus name

10. Every good thing stolen from my life while I shook hands with strange people, I recover you now, in Jesus name

11. My glory, depart from the location of setbacks in Jesus name

12. Every cobweb projection, targeted to make me poor, I refuse to be poor, in Jesus name

13. Every dark personality assigned to blow me out of existence, fall down and die in Jesus name

14. Blood of Jesus, silence every spider and cobweb scattering my favor and finances in Jesus' name.

15 Cobweb powers, disappear from my life in Jesus name.

16. Embargo of "you can't make it in life", placed upon my destiny through satanic spiders and cobwebs, be destroyed as I undertake this spiritual assignment in Jesus' name.

17. Every strongman using spiders and cobwebs to cause stagnation in my life, become powerless as I embark on this spiritual exercise.

18. Witchcraft cobwebs and spiders, confronting me day and night, be destroyed as I do this bath in Jesus' name.

19. Let the thunder of God locate and dismantle every witchcraft cobweb in my life and household.

20. Thank you Lord because you have answered my prayers, for in Jesus' name I pray. (AMEN)

CHAPTER FOUR

THE POWER OF EARLY MORNING URINE

Urine is a watery, typically yellowish, fluid stored in the bladder and discharged through the urethra. It is one of the body's chief means of eliminating excess water and salt, and it also contains nitrogen compounds such as urea and other waste substances removed from the blood by the kidneys. Urine is waste material that is secreted by the kidney. It is rich in end products such as urea, uric acid, and creatinine from protein metabolism, together with salts and pigments, and forms a clear amber and usually slightly acidic fluid.

In the spirit world, urine contains anti-witchcraft properties and powers that can neutralise witchcraft and demonic activities. This is why urine is also a very potent substance for combating witchcraft cobwebs and spiders. As useless as urine seems, it has colossal value in the spirit world. If you want to destroy any evil charm or enchantment against your life very fast, use your early morning urine.

However, in this chapter, we shall be looking at the spiritual benefits, uses, and functions of your early morning urine. Let's kick the ball rolling.

SPIRITUAL BENEFITS OF EARLY MORNING URINE

1. It breaks the stronghold of witchcraft spider and cobweb attacks in your life.

2. It prevents and protects you from witchcraft marks made on people's bodies at midnight.

3. It clears your path from evil blockage caused by demonic agents.

4. It removes witchcraft invisible marks from your body.

5. It prevents evil dreams and witchcraft manipulations from your life.

6. It drives evil spirits and witchcraft presence away from your houses and dwellings.

7. It prevents witchcraft monitoring spirit from monitoring your life and progress.

8. It often cancels out witchcraft spells as well as curses from devilish people.

9. It destroys generational curses.

10. It breaks the stronghold of stagnation and delay in your life.

12. It heals you of any spiritual injury or attack.

13. You become spiritually unavailable for destruction by the enemy.

14. It enhance career and business progress.

15. It destroys evil and satanic masks.

UNIQUE WAYS THROUGH WHICH YOUR EARLY MORNING URINE CAN BE USED TO ACHIEVE ALL OF THE ABOVE

(A) EARLY MORNING URINE HEAD AND FACE WASH

Instruction: *Carry out this spiritual assignment very early in the morning, precisely around 5:00 a.m. - 6:00 a.m. Do not talk to anyone before carrying out this assignment early in the morning. Do this exercise for 7 consecutive days. Also, never carry out this assignment during your period (monthly cycle) and abstain from sex during the period of this spiritual exercise.*

Needed Items: *Your early morning urine (the one you pass out, between 2:00 a.m. to 5:00 a.m), a container with which to take the urine.*

Procedure:

• Get a reasonable quantity of your early morning urine in a container without talking to anybody.

•The urine must be taken between 2:00 a.m. and 5:00 a.m.

• Keep the urine till around 5:30 a.m. to 6:00 a.m.

• Pray over the urine. (Ask God to sanctify it. Read Psalm 35 into the urine. Pray that the spiritual powers embedded in the human urine should work in your favour and destroy the works of the enemy in your life. Pray as led by the holy spirit).

• After praying very well, you wash your head and face with the urine without soap or sponge, while you continue to pray. Declare what you want as you rinse your head and face with the urine.

• Let the urine dry on your head and face. Let it spend up to 15-30 minutes before you wash it off and take your normal bath.

•Carry out this exercise for 7 consecutive days.

NOTE: •The urine may generate repulsive smell, don't worry. It is for the best. You can decide to stay away from people at this times to prevent possible embarrassment.

•If you don't live alone, let me teach you the easiest way to carry out this spiritual assignment.

• Get your early morning urine.

• *Pray into it and read Psalms 3, 24 and 35 into it.*

• *Go to the toilet, rinse your head and face with the urine without soap or sponge, while you continue to pray. Declare what you want as you rinse your head and face with the urine.*

• *Take a morning walk immediately in order to allow the urine to dry on your head and face without being in close contact with anyone.*

• *The early morning walk will prevent possible embarrassment the repulsive smell of the urine on your body might bring.*

• *After about 15-30 minutes walk, return home and heed straight to your bathroom to have your normal bath.*

• *God about your daily activities.*

• *Carry out this exercise for 7 consecutive days.*

By the grace of God, you will never experience cobweb or spider attacks again. Never! Till you die, you will never experience it again. This is another big mystery of God. The spiritual virtues that God has put in human urine are so powerful that witches and wizards can't demystify. When you do a urine head and face-wash regularly, it keeps evil and demonic people far from you.

The spiritual power in the urine, diffuses into your skin and body. Now, even at home or outside, evil people or people with bad intentions will always keep their distance from you. All spells and curses of evil and jealous people would be broken. When you observe a delay or stagnation in your life, try as quickly as you can to do urine head and face-wash.

Remember, I said you should speak into your life while rinsing your head and face with your urine. You need to offer prayer to God Almighty, who is the protector himself. It is God who puts power in your urine, so don't see the urine as your saviour. If you idolise it, God might hinder the whole process from working for you because God is a jealous God. You don't worship things created while you ignore the creator, who is the real source.

Whoever is secured by God has a guaranteed safety forever. So while taking your urine head and face-wash, open your mouth and pray, telling God what you want from him. God is too faithful to fail and will never fail you now. Amen.

(B) OTHER USES OF YOUR EARLY MORNING URINE

• *To remove negative energy around your house, shop, office, or business place, mix your early morning urine in water and spinkley around the premises. You can clean up* the water later on and use deodorant to quell the pungent smell.

• *If you notice that your finances are being attacked by witchcraft powers, get a small quantity of your early morning urine, and use it to rinse your hands without soap or sponge. Allow the water to dry on hands. Let the urine stay on your hands for 15-30minutes before washing it off. Do this repeatedly for 7 days, and you will see sporadic changes in your finances.*

NOTE: It is not medically advisable to drink your urine for whatever health or spiritual reason. Although, some advocate for urine therapy, but it is not proven to be safe medically. We should not, while trying to solve one problem create another for ourselves.

POSSIBLE PRAYER POINTS TO SUPPORT THE ABOVE SPIRITUAL ASSIGNMENTS

(Ask God for forgiveness of sins, the sins of your fathers, mothers and ancestors. Put your middle finger in the water and sanctify it in the name of Jesus).

1. I sanctify my urine for spiritual use this day in Jesus' name.

2. Lord, turn this urine into the blood of Jesus to destroy all works of Satan and witches in my life in Jesus' name.

3. I command your power of deliverance to enter this urine, such that as I use it to rinsey head and face, all Satanic cobweb and spider attacks will cease in Jesus' name.

4. I command the anti-evil power in this urine of mine to work for me and my deliverance in Jesus' name.

5. Evil powers that have vowed to bring me back to square through cobwebs and spiders receive total destruction in the name of Jesus through this urine.

6. Every ancestral cobwebs from my father's and mother's households, hiding my financial advancement from me, be destroyed as I go on this spiritual assignment in the name of Jesus.

7. Household witchcraft, confess and release my destiny now as I embark on this assignment in the name of Jesus.

8. Spirit of untimely death invoked against me from the kingdom of darkness through demonic spiders and cobwebs, go back to the sender now in the name of Jesus.

9. Blood of Jesus! Deliver me from satanic gridlock of spider and cobweb attacks, in Jesus' name.

10. Satanic cobwebs locking the warehouse of my blessings, be broken now as I embark on this spiri assignment in Jesus' name.

11. *Arrow of the Almighty God, target and destroy spiders and cobwebs troubling my life and my progress in life, in Jesus' name.*

12. *My original glory swallowed by demonic spiders and cobwebs, be freed, arise and locate me now, in Jesus name.*

13. *Every spider and cobweb veil covering my face, my progress and my life, wipe off as I carry out this divine instructions in Jesus' name.*

14. *Strange evil link from my foundation delaying my help, using spiders and cobwebs to instruct my glory, be disconnected as I do this spiritual exercise for the next 7 days in Jesus name.*

15. *Authority of darkness working against my urgent miracles through evil spiders and cobwebs, by authority of Jesus Christ through this spiritual exercise, stop it now, in Jesus' name.*

16. *Household enemies, hear me now, your activities shall not prosper in my life, in Jesus name.*

17. *Destroyer of glory, hear the word of the Lord, receive total destruction in Jesus name.*

18. *Every shadow of death following me, marking me for destruction through witchcraft spiders and cobwebs, disappear by the power in the blood of Jesus.*

19. You that spider and cobweb assigned against me I summon you for destruction, through this spiritual injunction, die, in Jesus' name.

20. I set myself free, you that spider and cobweb spirit, confronting me, receive divine destruction, in Jesus' name.

21. Thank you Lord because you have answered my prayers, for in Jesus' name I pray. (AMEN)

CHAPTER FIVE

THE POSITIVE AURAL AND CLEANSING PROPERTIES OF LEMON GRASS

(Cymbopogon citratus)

Cymbopogon citratus, also known as lemon grass, is a species of citronella grass or Cybophogon that grows to about two and a half metres. It has a pleasant scent or smell which resembles that of lemons, which is why it is popularly called lemon grass. It is often used as an insect repellent, especially for mosquitoes and houseflies.

Cymbophoto citratus, also known as lemon grass, is commonly cultivated as a culinary and medicinal herb in Africa and other parts of Asia. It is a plant that is native to

Africa, Madagascar, southern Asia, and the Bismarck Archipelago. It is naturalised in Polynesia, Hawaii, Mexico, Panama, the West Indies, Brazil, and Bolivia. In fact, India is the world's largest lemon grass grower, but this plant is also grown commercially in China, Malaysia, Thailand, Vietnam, and Guatemala.Other names of Cymbophoto Citratus according to different languages, tribes, and countries include the following:

It is called *"ewe tea" or "koriko oba" in Yoruba, "achara ehi" in Igbo, "Lemun tsami ciy" in Hausa, "ikonti" in Efik, "myoyaka" in Ibibio, "Tanglad" in the Philippines, "Hierba limon" in Spanish, "Capim-cidrao" or "Capim-santo" in Brazil, "Tej-sar" in Ethiopia, and "Citronelle" in French. It is called "Gandhabene" in India and "Cimbopogone" or "Citronella" in Italy. Lastly, it is called "Xiang Mao" in China.*

For thousands of years, lemon grass has always been prepared and taken as soups, curries, and teas. This plant is also said to carry immense health benefits. It is used in the preparation of a number of herbal medicines in many areas of Asia and Africa. Lemon grass, unfortunately, is not a member of the grass family, as its name implies. Instead, it is a perennial plant which grows in dense clumps of stiff and upright stems. Lemon grass grows from a rhizome, or bulb, but it doesn't tend to spread as much as some rhizomes can. Each clump of lemon grass can be up to 1.8 metres (6 feet) high and 1.2 metres (4 feet) wide.

Lemon grass is said to contain varieties of health benefits, as mentioned earlier, some of which include cleansing of the kidney, liver, pancreas, digestive and track bladder, reduction of blood pressure, detoxification of the body, anti oxidants, and the ability to stop diarrhoea and stomach aches, among other health benefits. But endeavour to seek the advice of your doctor before using lemon grass for health purposes.

If you live in an area or country where it is hard to find lemon grass, you can order some from Amazon, eBay, or other online stores across the world. Just search on Google and ask, "Where can I order lemon grass from?" and it will bring up a host of online stores where you can order from. The only difference is that it is the dried one that will be sent to you. But, whether dried or fresh, a lemon grass is a lemon grass. This doesn't diminish its efficacy and power.However, in this chapter, our main focus is not on the health benefits of lemon grass but on its spiritual uses and benefits. Our aim is to learn how we can explore the spiritual properties God has vested in this powerful plant to combat the works of Satan in our lives. They include the following:

SPIRITUAL BENEFITS OF CYMBOPOGON CITRATUS (LEMON GRASS)

1. It shields you from witchcraft spiders and cobweb attacks.

2. It prevents and protects you from witchcraft marks made on people's bodies overnight.

3. It clears your path from evil blockage by demonic agents.

4. It removes witchcraft invisible marks from your body.

5. It prevents evil dreams and witchcraft manipulations from your life.

6. It drives evil spirits and witchcraft presence away from your houses and dwellings.

7. It prevents witchcraft monitoring spirit from monitoring your life and progress.

8. It keeps evil people far from you.

9. It cancels out witchcraft spells as well as curses from devilish people.

10. It removes stagnation in your life.

11. It destroys the spirit of setbacks and backwardness.

12. It removes every mark of hatred from your body.

13. It removes evil energy from you and your dwelling.

14. It breaks the stronghold of marital delay. Suitors and prospective brides will just love you in an unexplainable way

15. It stops disappointment in your life.

16. It makes you visible to destiny helpers and they will have the desire to help you

17. It brings and causes favour and good-luck to you.

18. It mends people"s marriages and make their spouses love them the more.

19. It induces business and career success in you, i.e. increase in sales and patronage.

20. It shield you against false accusations from people.

21. It destroys generational curses.

22. It breaks the stronghold of stagnation and delay in your life.

23. It heals you of any spiritual injury or attack.

24. You become spiritually unavailable for destruction by the enemy.

UNIQUE WAYS THROUGH WHICH LEMON GRASS CAN BE USED TO ACHIEVE ALL OF THE ABOVE

(A) LEMON GRASS BATH

Instruction: *Carry out this spiritual assignment every night for 7 days. Do this assignment around 9:00.p.m when you are not going out again. Also, never carry out this assignment during your period (monthly cycle) and abstain from sex during the period of this spiritual exercise.*

Needed Items: *A reasonable quantity of fresh or dry lemon grass, water, cooking pot, cooking gas or stove, salt, a bathing bucket.*

Procedure:

• *Get a reasonable quantity of lemon grass.*

• *Rinse them in a clean water.*

• *Put them in a pot, add water (water that is enough to take a bath with).*

• *Put the pot which has the lemon grass and water on the fire.*

• *After that, add a table-spoon salt into the lemon grass and water.*

• *Boil for like 30 minutes.*

• *After boiling for 30 minutes, the water will change from white brownish colour, put the pot down, let the water cool off.*

• *Pour the boiled lemon grass water in an empty bucket (Do not additional water. That is why I said earlier that the water you put on the fire must be enough for you to bathe with)*

• *Read Psalms 24, 72 and Isaiah 60 into the lemon grass.*

• *Then pray into the water as led by the holy spirit (You can choose prayer points from those at the end of this chapter).*

• *After praying, take the lemon grass water to the bathroom for bath.*

• *Only rinse your entire body with the water, don't use soap or sponge.*

• *As you bathe with the water, speak into your life. Say the things you want and those you don't want. Ask God to make you immuned to Satanic spider and cobweb attacks and erase every evil mark of hatred on your body.*

• *After bathing, don't towel your body. Let the water dry on your body.*

• *While waiting for the lemon grass water to dry on your body, pray more and more.*

• *After the lemon grass water has dried up, you go to bed.*

• *Repeat the process for 7 days.*

By the grace of God, you will never experience cobweb or spider attacks again, plus, every mark of hatred on your body will be removed. This is a big mystery of God. The spiritual virtues that God puts in lemon grass are so powerful that witches and wizards can't fathom. When you bathe regularly with lemon grass water, it keeps evil people far from you.

The spiritual power of the lemon grass, which is contained in your bathing water, diffuses into your skin and body. Now, even at home or outside, evil people or people with bad intentions will always keep their distance from you. All spells and curses of evil and jealous people would be broken. When you observe a delay or stagnation in your life, try as quickly as you can to bathe with boiled lemon grass water.

Likewise, a boiled-lemon grass water bath heals you of any spiritual injury or attack from a person who does not mean any good for you. If you notice people just hate you for any reason, or your career or business is struggling, then you should seriously consider a lemon grass bath immediately. Do not wait until things get out of hand; prevention is better than cure.

Those who regularly bathe with lemon grass water wins the love and favour of everyone that they come in contact with.

When someone tries to attack you with unexplained hatred and disappointments, they will quickly find out that you are a no go area. This is because of your regular lemon grass bath. They will seek you but will not find you. This makes it impossible for them to harm you or hurt you spiritually and in any other way.

Remember, I said you should speak into your life while taking this bath. You need to offer prayer to God Almighty, who is the protector himself. It is God who puts power in the lemon grass, so don't see the leaf as your saviour. If you idolise the leaf, God might hinder the whole process from working for you because God is a jealous God. You don't worship things created while you ignore the creator, who is the real source.

Whoever is secured by God has a guaranteed safety forever. So while taking your bath, open your mouth and pray, telling God what you want from him. God is too faithful to fail and will never fail you now. Amen.

(B) OTHER USES OF LEMON GRASS

• *To remove negative energy around your house, shop, office, or business place, use boiled lemon grass water to mop the floor of your house, shop, office, or business place.*

• *To remove demonic and evil presence in your home, office, or business place, get dried lemons grass, if you* can't get dried one, get a fresh one and sun-dry it. Light a candle and burn the stands of the dried lemon grass one by one in the candle fire. The smoke removes evil and demonic presence in your home house and office. Let the smoke saturate every corner of your room and all demons will vanish. Do this consecutively for 7 days.

• When you constantly have evil dreams, keep an lemon grass in your room. Lemongrass can sometimes be a very powerful protective herb from evil presence and dreams.

• If you notice that your finances are being attacked by witchcraft powers, or your marriage is being attacked by demonic forces, get a small quantity of lemon grass. Put the leaves in a bottle of anointing oil (Olive oil). Pray on it daily for three days. Let it ferment very well. You can add fasting if you have the capacity to. Read Psalm 35 into it each day. On the third day, start using it. Use it to rub your palms and head every morning. Your head signifies your glory. You will notice a drastic change in your finances and marriage after this exercise. You will discover that your husband or wife will love you more and you both will make up and stop quarrelling. You both will each other more and live happily ever after.

POSSIBLE PRAYER POINTS TO SUPPORT THE ABOVE SPIRITUAL ASSIGNMENTS

(Ask God for forgiveness of sins, the sins of your fathers, mothers and ancestors. Put your middle finger in the water and sanctify it in the name of Jesus).

1. Lord, forgive all my sins, sins of my mother, father and ancestors which may be opening me up for Satanic oppression in Jesus' name.

2. I sanctify this lemon grass water with the name of Jesus and I ask that it turns into the blood of Jesus destroying every works of Satan in my life.

3. I command every household strongman using cobweb to block my way and cause me inexplicable hatred be destroyed as I carry out this spiritual exercise in Jesus' name.

4. Every witchcraft spider flying contrary to my destiny, causing me promise and fail, rise and fall and general disappointment, fall down and die as I undertake this bath in Jesus' name.

5. I release myself from every curse of cobwebs and spiders working against me and my destiny in the name of Jesus.

6. Every wicked spider and cobweb installed against me and my destiny be overthrown as I undertake this spiritual exercise in the name of Jesus.

7. Every agent of spider and cobweb working against my life and destiny, fall down and die in the name of Jesus.

8. Every satanic spider and cobweb delegated to covering my way and glory, causing me hardship and stagnancy be destroyed in the name of Jesus.

9. Every hostile and wicked person imprisoning my wealth and glory through cobwebs and spiders I bind you in the name of Jesus.

10. Every cobweb arrester, arresting my goodness, glory and destiny, receive divine blindness in the name of Jesus.

11. Every power of spider and cobweb, blocking my physical and spiritual growth and progress, fall down and die in Jesus' name.

12. Every power rearranging and reshuffling my problems through spiders and cobweb attacks, fall down and die in Jesus' name.

13. Every power of spider and cobweb contributing stubbornness to my problem and energising my battle, fall down and die in Jesus' name.

14. I refuse to be diverted from the path of blessing and destiny through demonically sponsored cobwebs and spiders in the name of Jesus.

15. *Every cobweb and spiders resident in my head, hands, face, body, feet, mouth, be destroyed as I embark on this spiritual assignment in Jesus' name.*

16. *Every trap set for me through spiders and cobwebs, begin to catch your owners in the name of Jesus.*

17. *Every spider and cobweb padlock closed against my life, destiny, finances, marriage, academics, and in any other area of my life, be destroyed as I undertake this spiritual exercise.*

18. *I break myself loose from every bondage and covenant of spiders and cobwebs made by me or in my behalf in the name of Jesus.*

19. *Every spider and cobweb coffin where any of my glory, virtues, goodness and blessings are hidden and buried, be exhumed as I embark on this spiritual assignment in Jesus' name.*

20. *Every evil ever done to me through cobweb and spider attack be reversed in the name of God the Father, God the Son, and God the Holy Spirit as i embark on this spiritual instruction in Jesus' name.*

21. *Thank you Lord because you have answered my prayers, for in Jesus' name I pray. (AMEN)*

CHAPTER SIX

LAST WORD

Come unto me, all you that labour and are heavy laden, and I will give you rest. Take my yoke upon you, and learn of me; for I am meek and lowly in heart: and you shall find rest unto your souls. For my yoke is easy, and my burden is light.

Matthew 11:28-30 (KJV)

Above all, accepting Jesus Christ into your life is very important so that you have eternal life after fighting and winning all of life's battles. It will be sad to be successful here on earth while losing one's soul to hell. The idea is for us to live and have a heaven-on-earth experience here on earth and, at the same time, go to heaven to continue the enjoyment.

Another version of the bible verse above says, *"Are you tired? Worn out? Burned out on religion? Come to me. Get away with me, and you'll recover your life. I'll show you how to take a real rest. Walk with me and work with me—watch how I do it. Learn the unforced rhythms of grace. I won't lay anything heavy or ill-fitting on you. Keep company with me, and you'll learn to live freely and lightly."* I have no iota of doubt in me that demonic spider and cobweb attacks confronting your life will become a thing of the past after reading this book and carrying out all the spiritual instructions outlined in it. Jesus Christ deliberately inspired me to write this book so as to help set captives free, captives who have been under the demonic oppression of cobwebs and spiders attacks for many years.

Jesus has come to destroy the works of Satan, as stated in **1 John 3:8 (KJV)** ..."*He that committeth sin is of the devil; for the devil sinneth from the beginning. For this purpose, the Son of God was manifested, that he might destroy the works of the devil.*" Jesus has come to counter the three (3) point demonic agenda of Satan, which are to steal, kill, and destroy, as outlined in **John 10:10 (KJV)** ... "*The thief cometh not, but for to steal, and to kill, and to destroy; I am come that they might have life, and that they might have it more abundantly.*"

It will be my desire that you give your life to Jesus Christ so that you can live an oppression-free life and enjoy a life of heaven on earth here on earth *(pun not intended, smiles).* If you have not given your life to Christ before, or you have not properly done so before, or perhaps, you backslided after many tribulations, here is an opportunity to do so. So that we can all meet in heaven to further celebrate our victories both here on earth and in heaven. If you have not given your life to Christ before or you want to re-dedicate your life to Christ, simply say the following prayer with me:

"

Lord Jesus, I accept you into my life today to stir the ship of my life. I have suffered too long at the hands of the devil and his agents. Forgive me all my sins and create in me a new heart. You changed the lives and stories of many people in the past; don't let my own be different. I want you to change my story too. Put all my enemies to shame and those who mock me every day, thinking nothing good can come out of my life. Disappoint those who believe I cannot be free from their oppression. Let them end up bowing before me and apologising. In the end, let me reign with you in your kingdom. In Jesus' name, I pray. (Amen).

"

P. S: *For further spiritual help and counselling, send an email to the author on the email address: s.treasure12@gmail.com.*

FOR FURTHER SPIRITUAL COUNSELING, HELP & SUPPORT

Visit the headquarters of any Celestial Church of Christ nearest to you. Our times of service are as follows:

OUR TIMES OF SERVICE

Tuesday: •Spiritual Consultation

Wednesday: •Mercy Service •Evening Congregational Service

Friday: •Prophets & Prophetesses Service •Service for the Pregnant Women •Evening Power Service

Sunday: Morning Congregational Service

SUPPLEMENTARY PRAYER POINTS

1. Holy Ghost fire, burn to ashes every cobweb that will not allow good things to locate me in Jesus' name.

2. My Father, let any man or woman of darkness using cobwebs as a means to enter my life, Holy Ghost fire frustrate them, in the name of Jesus.

3. Satanic cobwebs attack meant to render me out of favour, I set you on fire, burn to ashes, in. the name of Jesus.

4. Cobweb attack of evil re-enforcements and destiny killers, waiting for me at the season of my blessings; receive fire, burn to ashes, in the. name of Jesus.

5. I command every demonic cobweb placed upon my hands, legs, head, neck and waist to break by fire, in the name of Jesus.

6. My Father, Let any strange man or woman manipulating my life and marital destiny with cobwebs, be destroyed, in the name of Jesus.

7. My Father, let every witchcraft cobweb from any stubborn personality in my household, be roasted by fire, in the name of Jesus.

8. *Every satanic cobweb assign to divert me from the path of my breakthrough, be consumed by Holy Ghost fire, in the name of Jesus.*

9. *Cobweb of no way!!! set against my blessings and favour, receive fire, burn to ashes, in the name of Jesus.*

10. *Powers of my father's house and mother's house that are sending invisible cobweb against me, I bind you with Holy Ghost fire, in the name of Jesus.*

11. *Witchcraft cobweb covering my glory from being noticed by my helpers, Catch fire, loose your hold over me completely, in the name of Jesus.*

12. *Holy Ghost fire, destroy every strongman using cobweb to harass the glory of my family, in the name of Jesus.*

13. *Cobweb attack of missed opportunity attacking me day and night, I set you on fire, in the name of Jesus.*

14. *Every evil ever done to me through cobweb attacks, be reversed by fire, in the name of Jesus.*

15. *Let the thunder of God locate and dismantle every witchcraft power using cobweb to fire afflictions into my life, in the name of Jesus.*

16. Any sin that my parents and ancestors committed, that gave room for spiritual attacks to operate fully in my life, be washed away by the blood of Jesus.

17. Every power that want me to die in this condition, you are a liar, die, in Jesus name

18. Every dark power that is monitoring me, receive blindness in Jesus name

19. Every power assigned to change my destiny, die, in Jesus name

20. Every good thing stolen from my life while I shook hands with strange spirit, I recover you now, in Jesus name

21. My glory, depart from the location of setbacks in Jesus name

22. I refuse to be poor, in Jesus name

23. I refuse to live a life of spiritual attacks, in Jesus name

24. Dark personality assigned to blow me out of existence, fall down and die in Jesus name.

25. Household cobweb attacking the glory of my head, catch fire, in the name of Jesus.

26. Arrows from the wicked foundation against my progress, go back to the sender, in Jesus name.

27. Evil cobweb of blockage, I am not your candidate, clear by fire and catch fire by thunder, in the name of Jesus.

28. Cobweb of non-achievement, operating against me from my family line, disappear by fire by force in Jesus name.

29. Cobweb of no way, set against my favor and helpers receive fire, burn to ashes.

30. Household spiders on my face, catch fire, in the name of Jesus.

31. Any man or woman using cobweb as an access to enter my life, fall and die, in the name of Jesus.

32. Right hand on your head: Every cobweb spirit attached to my life, I bind and cast you out, in Jesus name.

33. Let every net of demonic cobweb placed upon my head be consumed by fire in Jesus name.

34. I command every demonic chain of cobweb placed upon my hands, legs, neck and waist to break and be melted by fire, in the name of Jesus

DROP A REVIEW

If you found this book helpful, kindly drop a review to help create awareness about it. Your review will go a long way to convince others to buy and benefit too. To write your review, visit the link below and click on the book to write your honest review:

https://www.amazon.com/dp/B0CYTMWNDM

For Prayers, Spiritual help, Counselling, Clarifications, Questions and other Enquiry, contact the author on +2348067009303 (WhatsApp) or email gtreasure35@gmail.com.

Many Thanks.

ABOUT THE AUTHOR

S. G Treasure is a world renowned Life-Coach and Novelangelist. He has authored many books on faith, relationship, marriage, parenting, career, finances, and human capacity development. He runs an encouragement ministry dedicated to encouraging people going through tough and difficult times around the world.

Visit the link below to view other books written by the author:

https://www.amazon.com/author/sg_treasure

OTHER HELPFUL BOOKS BY THE AUTHOR

✓ **THE ENCOURAGEMENT HANDBOOK FOR THE DEPRESSED & DOWNCAST:**
A Compendium of 15 Powerful Encouragement Write-ups that will Launch You out of Depression, Loneliness, Hopelessness & Despair

Description: Tough times are indispensable to everyone who breathes. Likewise, life is an uncertain roller coaster full of ups and downs. Everybody goes through difficult times, but how we manage and respond to challenges differentiates us from one another. Those who persevere and push through those difficult moments eventually become successful.

In view of this, the book**, "THE ENCOURAGEMENT HANDBOOK FOR THE DEPRESSED & DOWNCAST"** has been published. The book has been written to help those going through one hard time or the other push through and overcome. The book offers everyone going through tough and difficult times all the support, comfort and solace that they need, with the assurance that they will overcome. It is an encouragement companion (handbook) which reminds it's readers on daily basis that they are not alone. The book contains 15 powerful, God inspired and solution driven write-ups capable of bringing every depressed and hopeless person back life, and on their feet again with top of the world smiles.

Book length- 121 pages

To get a copy of the book, visit the link below:

https://www.amazon.com/dp/B0C8ZM6GBY

✓ THE REJECTED STONE

Amazing Stories of Rejected Men & Women Who Later Became Successful Despite all Odds

Description: Rejection' can be referred to as a state of being unwanted or non-acceptance of one's beliefs, opinions, or ideas by others. It is a state of being abandoned, disowned, or ostracised by loved ones. Rejection is one social problem that has caused many people serious emotional and psychological problems. It has bred low self-esteem, self-pity, a lack of self-confidence, and possibly suicide in many people.

As a result of this, the book **"THE REJECTED STONE"** has been written. The book has been published to help victims of rejection overcome the scourge, while bouncing back to becoming 'chief cornerstones' in their careers, academics, and other areas of life. It has been put together to help victims turn rejection into a stepping stone rather than a stumbling block on their path to success. Consequently, everyone struggling with rejection *(in whatever area of life)* will find this book a useful self-help spiritual guide that brings one out of social rejection into social prominence and acceptance. Welcome on board!

Book length- 121 pages

To get a copy of the book, visit the link below:

https://www.amazon.com/dp/B0CSKNY1P3

✓ OVERCOMING LONELINESS & SOLITUDE AT YOUTHFUL & OLD AGE:

Building Healthy Social Relationships & Lonely-Free Life

Description: Loneliness is a feeling of unwanted isolation *(whether physical or psychological)* aided by lack of social connection with others. It is a state of having no intimate friend or companion which leaves one sad. It is a very dangerous emotion which can aid or fuel the most lethal psychological and health problems anyone can have. Loneliness remains one of the shortest cuts to depression as it fuels over thinking, high blood pressure, cardiovascular problems as well as other deadly diseases. It kills its victims slowly, making it one of the greatest enemies of man.

In view of this, the book, **"OVERCOMING LONELINESS AND SOLITUDE AT YOUTHFUL AND OLD AGE"** has been written. The book has been published to help victims of loneliness overcome the scourge. The book offers its readers working practical solutions to overcoming loneliness both at youthful and old age. The book contains **seven chapters** which thoroughly demystify the *meaning, types, symptoms, causes, effects and way out* of loneliness. Consequently, everyone struggling with loneliness, *(whether situational or chronic)* will find this book a useful self-help guide which brings one out of solitude into social prominence. Welcome on board!

Book length- 151 pages

To get a copy of the book, visit the link below:

https://www.amazon.com/dp/B0C9S8W3CR

✓ HOW NOT TO LOVE A MAN:

12 Love Gestures Single Ladies Exhibit Which Kill Men's Love for them"

Description: One might be wondering why a single lady, after attracting a good man, is unable to keep such a man on a long term basis. The reason for this is not far fetched. There are many innocent love gestures single women exhibit in relationships which kill men's love for them. If these innocent love behaviours are left unaddressed, they could become a long-term cog in the wheel of relationship progress for any woman. Men are wired up differently and lack of this understanding can make a woman innocently destroy her partner's romantic feelings for her without even knowing.

In view of this, the book, **"HOW NOT TO LOVE A MAN:***12 Love Gestures Single Ladies Exhibit Which Kill Men's Love for them*" has been published. The book has been written to educate single ladies on 12 romantic gestures that they exhibit which kill men's love for them. Therefore, single ladies, who desire to have their love affairs taken to the next level within a very short time, will find this book highly beneficial, helpful and irresistible. Welcome on board!

Book length- 90 pages

To get a copy of the book, visit the link below:

https://www.amazon.com/dp/B0CFCX6X7D

✓ HOW TO MAKE FRIENDS AT SCHOOL

Secrets of Building Healthy Social Relationships in High School, College or the University

Description: A number of high school and college level students have difficulty making friends at school which may have a negative impact on their physical, emotional and psychological well-being. According to research, a healthy social life in school can encourage positive learning attitudes as well as improved academic performance, while a poor one may lead to academic underachievement or complete withdrawal from school. Friends met either at high school or college can play a positive role in shaping young people's lives and future. Sometimes, friends can be a stepping stone to achieving greatness in life.

In view of this, the book, **"HOW TO MAKE FRIENDS IN SCHOOL"** has been written. The book has been published to help high school and college level students make friends and build social connection in school with relative ease. The book shares about **nine (9) hindrances** which prevent school learners from building healthy social lives, as well as **twenty-eight (28) steps** to building quality friendships and lasting social relationships in school. Consequently, high school, college level or university students, who find social connection with fellow students a herculean task, will find this book useful, helpful and highly irresistible. Welcome on board!

Book length- 95 pages

To get a copy of the book, visit the link below:

https://www.amazon.com/dp/B0CLHZRR1R

✓ HOW TO MAKE FRIENDS IN 120 SECONDS

Top Secrets of Building Quality Friendship & Social Relationship with Anyone

Description: A healthy social life is very key to the physical, emotional and psychological well-being of humans. According to research, a healthy social life tends to bring happiness, good health, sense of belonging and a healthy self-esteem to people, while a poor one may lead to loneliness, anxiety, depression and other lethal health challenges. Social connection is indispensable to humans, as it creates a feeling of fulfillment, happiness and belongingness in people. Friends can also play a positive role in shaping an individual's life and future.

In view of this, the book, **"HOW TO MAKE FRIENDS IN 120 SECONDS"** has been written. The book has been published to help individuals who find social connection with others a nail-biting or head-scraching experience to do so with relative ease. The book shares about **twenty (20) steps and strategies** which can help an individual build quality friendship with anyone in just 120 seconds. It also shares about **nine (9) major hindrances** to building a healthy social life at home, at work, at school and at other strategic places. Consequently, individuals, who find social connection with other a herculean task, will find this book useful, helpful and highly irresistible. Welcome on board!

Book length- 96 pages

To get a copy of the book, visit the link below:

https://www.amazon.com/dp/B0CLYB3NMD

✓ KILL LONELINESS BEFORE IT KILLS YOU

Over 20 Health Consequences of Loneliness & Ways to Overcome

Description: Loneliness, being an inimical social and emotional problem must be stopped before it "stops" its victims. It can be defined as a feeling of unwanted isolation (whether physical or psychological) aided by lack of social connection with others. Loneliness is a state of having no intimate friend or companion which leaves one sad. It is a very dangerous emotion which can aid or fuel most lethal psychological and health problems anyone can have.

Fortunately, in the book **"KILL LONELINESS BEFORE IT KILLS YOU"**, the author peruses over 20 health implications of loneliness and ways to overcome the scourge. The book has been published to help victims of loneliness overcome the menace while living better and happier lives. The book also offers working practical solutions to overcoming loneliness with its attendant health implications. Consequently, everyone struggling with the deadly emotion called "loneliness" will find this book a useful self-help guide which brings one out of solitude into social prominence. Welcome on board!

Book length- 105 pages

To get a copy of the book, visit the link below:

https://www.amazon.com/dp/B0CP93KF27

✓ HOW TO BUILD YOUR PUBLIC SPEAKING CONFIDENCE : *A Guide to Speaking Publicly without Fear or Apprehension*

Description: Lack of public speaking confidence is one social problem that has grounded many careers, dreams, and aspirations. The social problem, also known as 'glossophobia', is not unconnected to the fear of being scrutinised and ridiculed for making speech error(s) in front of a large audience. Yet, the ability to speak confidently in public is one social skill that everyone should and must possess, whether now or later in life.

In view of this, the book **"HOW TO BUILD YOUR PUBLIC SPEAKING CONFIDENCE"** has been written. The book has been published to help individuals who find public speaking a fearful and dreaded venture overcome their fears while, in the process, becoming confident and impeccable public speakers. The book peruses over 20 strategies to help readers build the confidence that they need to excel in the business of public speaking. However, everyone who finds public speaking a nail-biting and head-scratching experience due to glossophobia will find this book highly useful, helpful, and irresistible. Welcome on board!

Book length - 80 pages

To get a copy of the book, visit the link below:

https://www.amazon.com/dp/B0CPWS17CR

✓ THE PRINCIPLE OF SITTING BY IT:

How to Nurture Your Prayer Seeds Into Bountiful Harvests

Description: The greatest tragedy on earth is not death, but virtues, wealth, resources, treasures, and blessings being trapped in heaven's treasury while the beneficiaries languish in poverty, pain, sickness, barrenness, loneliness, and unfruitfulness here on earth.When some people get to heaven and see the enormous wealth and goodies they were supposed to enjoy here on earth, which never reached them, they will weep, weep, and weep. In view of this, the book **"THE PRINCIPLE OF SITTING BY IT"** has been written. The book has been published to help Christians nurture their prayer seeds into bountiful harvests on one hand and to help release many believers' trapped and hijacked blessings in the heavenlies.

The book contains about **nine (9) spiritual nutrients** and weapons which can help nurture your prayer seeds into bountiful harvests as well as release all trapped blessings from heaven's treasury. Consequently, everyone desiring instant, immediate, and secured answers to their prayers will find this book a very useful spiritual guide which forcefully releases one's heavenly trapped blessings for earthly use. Welcome on board!

Book length- 90 pages

To get a copy of the book, visit the link below:

https://www.amazon.com/dp/B0CV44G9SJ

✓ YOUR HOUR OF DELIVERANCE HAS COME:

Deliverance from Poverty, Sickness, Barrenness, Marital Failure, Stagnation and Every Demonic Oppression

Description: The hour has come for the those kept under the oppression of the devil to be set free. The hour for freedom from poverty, sickness, barrenness, marital failure, stagnation and every demonic oppression has come! Many are suffering from heavy satanic oppression that they don't even know what else to do to gain their freedom, but I want to tell you that that hour has come for the lord to liberate you. Whatever captivity the enemy may have put you, whether in your finances, career, health, marriage, reproductive life or academics,, I see the lord setting you free right now.in Jesus' name!

The book **"YOUR HOUR OF DELIVERANCE HAS COME"** is a holy spirit inspired book written to break all forms of curses and chains of the enemy in your life. The book has seven (7) chapters and each chapter peruses spiritual steps needed to be taken to be permanently free from all the oppressions of the devil. Consequently, everyone suffering from one oppression of the devil or another will will find this book very helpful, useful and handy.

Book length- 60 pages

To get a copy of the book, visit the link below:

https://www.amazon.com/dp/B0CW1NJV47

BIBLIOGRAPHY

https://en.m.wiktionary.org/wiki/spider

https://en.m.wiktionary.org/wiki/spiders

https://en.m.wikipedia.org/wiki/Spider

https://simple.m.wikipedia.org/wiki/Spider

https://simple.m.wiktionary.org/wiki/cobweb

https://en.m.wiktionary.org/wiki/cobweb

https://en.m.wiktionary.org/wiki/cobwebs

https://en.m.wikipedia.org/wiki/Cobweb_(disambiguation)

https://en.m.wikipedia.org/wiki/Spider_web

https://simple.m.wikipedia.org/wiki/Spider_web

https://en.m.wiktionary.org/wiki/spiderweb

https://en.m.wiktionary.org/wiki/spider-web

https://en.m.wikipedia.org/wiki/Ocimum_gratissimum

https://en.m.wikibooks.org/wiki/Cookbook:Scent_Leaf

https://en.m.wikipedia.org/wiki/Basil

https://en.m.wikipedia.org/wiki/List_of_culinary_herbs_and_spices

https://m.wikidata.org/wiki/Q2355390

https://m.wikidata.org/wiki/Q104063498

https://en.m.wiktionary.org/wiki/Lantana_camara

https://en.m.wiktionary.org/wiki/lantana

https://m.wikidata.org/wiki/Q332469

https://en.m.wikipedia.org/wiki/Lantana_camara

https://en.m.wikipedia.org/wiki/File:Twin_lantana_camara_edit.jpg

https://commons.m.wikimedia.org/wiki/File:Lantana_camara_3.jpg

https://commons.m.wikimedia.org/wiki/File:Lantana_camara.jpg

https://en.m.wiktionary.org/wiki/urine

https://simple.m.wiktionary.org/wiki/urine

https://en.m.wiktionary.org/wiki/urinate

https://en.m.wikipedia.org/wiki/Urine

https://en.m.wikipedia.org/wiki/Urine_therapy

https://en.m.wiktionary.org/wiki/urine_therapy

https://en.m.wiktionary.org/wiki/urine_therapies

https://m.wikidata.org/wiki/Q606754

https://en.m.wikipedia.org/wiki/Urophagia

https://en.m.wiktionary.org/wiki/lemongrass

https://en.m.wikipedia.org/wiki/Cymbopogon

https://en.m.wikipedia.org/wiki/Cymbopogon_citratus

https://en.m.wikipedia.org/wiki/LemonGrass_(band)

https://en.m.wikipedia.org/wiki/Cymbopogon_citratus

https://en.m.wikipedia.org/?redirect=no&title=Lemongra ss

https://en.m.wikipedia.org/wiki/Lemongrass_(disambigua tion)

https://en.m.wikipedia.org/wiki/Urine_therapy

Notes

Notes

Notes

Notes

Notes

Notes

_____

_____

_____

_____

_____

_____

_____

_____

_____

_____

_____

_____

_____

_____

_____

Notes

Notes

_____

_____

_____

_____

_____

_____

_____

_____

_____

_____

_____

_____

_____

_____

_____

_____

Notes

Notes

_____

_____

_____

_____

_____

_____

_____

_____

_____

_____

_____

_____

_____

_____

_____

_____

Made in the USA
Las Vegas, NV
28 May 2024

90475327R00066